The
Hidden
Code of God

(Nature's Natural Bible of Free Will)

Matthew McNeil Asher

ISBN 978-1-64300-005-3 (Paperback)
ISBN 978-1-64300-006-0 (Digital)

Copyright © 2018 Matthew McNeil Asher
All rights reserved
First Edition

Covenant Books, Inc.
11661 Hwy 707
Murrells Inlet, SC 29576
www.covenantbooks.com

THE HIDDEN CODE OF GOD

**THIS IS NOT MY OPINION AND IT IS NOT A FACT.
THE CHOICE IS YOURS.
DECLARATION OF INDEPENDENCE.**

Inalienable Rights of Free Will of Freedom.

Endowed by creator Natural Law	Human Rights = Freedom = Water or Inalienable Rights = Free Will = H_2O Individual	Endowed by destroyer Unnatural Law
1. Life–Fight for 2. Liberty 3. Pursuit of happiness, What they want or What they do Executive power (they pray to grow)	No free will–Free choice No freedom in land or domain of free land	1. Pursuit of happiness, What they want or What they do Executive power (the predators) 2. Liberty 3. Life–Flight from

---

Prehistoric Law of Nature
The Thinking Process is Before Action

1. Life	1. Pursuit of Action to survive
2. Liberty	2. Liberty
3. Pursuit of Action to survive	3. Life

UNDER THE LAW   ABOVE THE LAW

Who put these in order of checks and balances of law	These are called Low–Life's. They put life last.
1. Christt ⟵	⟶ 1. Hitler
2. Gandhi ⟵	⟶ 2. Stalin
3. Martin Luther King	3. Slavery
4. Firefighters	4. Pyromaniacs
5. Heroes	5. Terrorists
6. Doctors Good | Evil	6. Murderers
7. Pharmacy	7. Drug Cartel
8. Most Police Officers	8. Criminals
9. Hope	9. Suicide
10. Life	10. Extinction
11. America Today	11. North Korea today
12. Peace	12. War

The only good ones on this side are the
-Dare
-Devils

Mostly with   The List Goes   **The Line**   The List Goes   Mostly without
faith in God   On To Life.   **Between**   On To   faith in God
or Human Life.   **Good & Evil.**   Extinction.   or Human Life.

3

Three–Trinity within unity
Under the Law – (Law made easy)

1. Life (Brackets of Law)

2. Liberty (includes property & body)

3. Pursuit of what you want or do for happiness, or survival

---

1. Regulations for debate within the community of the pursuit of happiness

Branch–Pursuit Branch

Regulations   Ex.   1. Loud Music
                       2. Smoking laws
                       3. Etc.

---

1. Nothing broken
2. Nothing broken
3. Nothing broken
4. ART
5. Music
6. School
7. Work
8. Travel
9. Sports–Legal
10. Other that could not be listed

Three–Trinity without unity
Above the Law

1. Pursuit of action (Broken brackets of Law)

2. Liberty to protect the persons pursuit of action

3. Life of others last

$$\left(\begin{array}{c}\text{Some only take}\\\text{liberty, not life}\end{array}\right) - \left(\begin{array}{c}\text{Above the law}\\\text{low lives}\end{array}\right)$$

---

1. Red Light running
2. Drunk driving
3. Shoplifting
4. Breaking and Entering
5. Assault
6. Bank robbery
7. Identity theft
8. Copyright Infringement
9. Plagiarism
10. Property theft
11. Home invasion
12. Murder
13. Manslaughter
14. Rape
15. Stalking
16. Public or private food tampering
17. Kidnapped
18. Illegal Drug Sales
19. Blackmail – Frauds – Scams
20. Others that could not be listed

Bible Code

1) Life—Process of making or saving life.
2) Liberty.
3) Pursuit of happiness or action. = Power.

These are only sins,
not both crimes
and sins.
Only lightly persuaded,
Never to be punished
but not rewarded.

1) Pursue of happiness or action. = Power.
2) Liberty.
3) Life (Process of making or saving life).

Saint   Sin   (This is the power over life)
                                                                     It's about the power over life

Life Above the power   ## The power over life

1) Life or survival. ....→ 1) Suicide and or assisted in suicide.

2) No condom use. ....→ 2) Condom use.

3) Protect life of developing human being. ....→3) Abortion.

4) No pill or Morning After pill. ....→ 4) The use of pill or Morning After pill.

5) Abstinence. ....→5) Masturbation.

6) Research without killing cells of life or destroying life. ....→ 6) Stem cell research with life not. Preserved.

7) Have as many children that happens naturally. ....→ 7) Population control like in China.

8) Unity of marriage that matches the possibility of producing life. ....→ 8) Sexual acts or relations that do not preserve life or make natural life outside of the bond of life.

9) Monogamy with wife or husband within the bond of protecting life. ....→ 9) Cheating on wife or husband outside bond of preserving and protecting life.

10) More to come.   10) More to come.

FORMULA TEXT OF HUMANITY

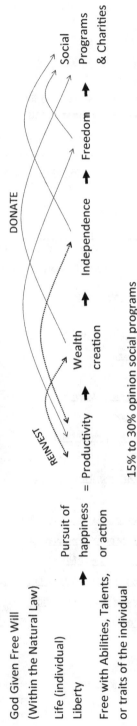

God Given Free Will
(Within the Natural Law)

Life (individual)
Liberty
Pursuit of happiness = Productivity or action
Free with Abilities, Talents, or traits of the individual

Productivity → Wealth creation → Independence → Freedom → Social Programs & Charities

DONATE
REINVEST

15% to 30% opinion social programs

Lets Flip the Formula Upside Down Like Cuba

Government Given Free Will
(Outside of Natural Law)
Social Programs

Less Liberty Restricted abilities, talents and traits.

Less productivity → Less wealth creation → Less Independence More Dependence → Less Freedom Overall → More social programs with less quality of care & charities suffer

The relationship between government and the citizen becomes a father-child relationship. Rather than a relationship like a marriage or spouse to spouse.

Destruction of the church is very important to eliminate competition of the government to put social programs first. Sometimes if the government can't destroy the church they (government) destroy the structure of the family. This is to put the individual alone and to make him/her more dependent on the government power.

When the cause becomes more important than the truth (The one life), The individual inalienable rights become less important than the group. In other words if you don't protect the one you can't protect the whole.

Checks and Balances of American Law & Order

Structure   of   America

Trinity within unity

1. Free Will—Individual Rights

1) Life
2) Liberty
3) The pursuit of what you want to do

$\left.\right\}$ = $\dfrac{\text{This is an equation to get a result}}{\text{For individual}}$

2. Community

1) Life—Child or Children—Life
2) Family—Mother/Father—or other choices—Liberty
3) Community—Support Groups—City Council—Pursuit

3.

1) Local Judicial Representative—Life
2) Police & Fire Department—Law that's made—Liberty
3) City Council—Regulators—Pursuit

4.

1) Legislative—People Life—Life
2) Judicial—Liberty Branch—Law Branch—Liberty
3) Executive Branch—Pursuit of Action from the Voters and that did not vote.—Pursuit

5.

F | Federal Selective Best -Life— People or Branch—Life

B | Liberty (talk reason logic) - Liberty—of Law—Liberty

I | Pursuit of Action of Results- Info—of Law—Pursuit

6.

D | Department of Best People—for Branch—Life

O | Reason Logic Law—Conclusion—within Law—Liberty

J | Results Pursuit of Action and Conclusion of Justice

 | within Law—Pursuit

7.

C | Life—Team—Best People Branch—Life

I | Liberty—Mission Reason Logic—of mission—Liberty

A | Pursuit of Action—Results of Mission—Data—Pursuit

National Slogan

1) Truth—Life

2) Justice—Liberty

3) American—Way of pursuit

- These can NOT be broken or Law is broken
- 3 checks and balances of Justice and Law and Order of the brackets

Code of Logic

Ace—Life

King—Liberty (Your Rights) Queen—

Pursuit of Action or What you Do

Also, FDA, EPA, DOD, IRS, ICE, HUD, CBP, Some have 4—5 letters

---

Checks & Balances

Light Speed—Physics Universe—Matter of Stuff

Life Creation—Liberty of Creatures in Universe—Pursuit of Action of Creatures

One cannot go over the other just like the Constitution and Law & Order. Things will fall apart.

$NL > M > ORG^2 >$ Life, liberty, and the pursuit of action or happiness.

THIS IS NOT MY OPINION AND IT IS NOT A FACT.
THE CHOICE IS YOURS.
DECLARATION OF INDEPENDENCE.

Formula of Life

"At His Best, Man is the Noblest of all Animals.
Separated from Law and Justice, He is the Worst."
— Aristotlo

At his best, Man is the Noblest of All Animals.

Law = Life
Justice = The order of the Liberty
To protect Law and order Life and Liberty

So we can be safe pursuing our happiness.

Human Rights =
Freedom = Water or
Inalienable Rights =
Free Will = H_2O
of Individuals freedom
They are the same thing.

Man separated from Law and Justice can be the worst.

(Outside of Law and Life or the order of Justice of Life & Liberty).

1. Life—Fight for

2. Liberty

3. Pursuit of happiness,
   What they want or
   What they do

1. Pursuit of happiness,
   What they want or
   What they do

2. Liberty

3. Life—Flight from

UNDER THE LAW

Who put these in order of checks and balances of law

1. Christ
2. Gandhi
3. Martin Luther King
4. Firefighters
5. Heroes
6. Doctors
7. Pharmacy
8. Most Police Officers
9. Hope
10. Life
11. America Today
12. Peace

ABOVE THE LAW

These are called Low—Life's.
They put life last.

1. Hitler
2. Stalin
3. Slavery
4. Pyromaniacs
5. Terrorists
6. Murderers
7. Drug Cartel
8. Criminals
9. Suicide
10. Extinction
11. North Korea today
12. War

The only good ones on this side are the
-Dare
-Devils

Mostly with
faith in God
or Human Life.

The Line
Between

Mostly without
faith in God
or Human Life.

Three–Trinity
Under the Law – (Law made easy)

"At his Best, Man is the Noblest of all Animals". – Aristotle

(Inside Law and Order)

↓

1. Life (Brackets of Law)

2. Liberty (includes property & body)
   (Order of Justice)

3. Pursuit of what you want or do
   (Happiness) or action
   (Respect for Human Life)

_____

1. Regulations for debate within
   the community of the pursuit of
   happiness

Branch–Pursuit Branch

	Ex.	1. Loud Music
Regulations		2. Smoking laws
		3. Etc.

_____

1. Nothing broken
2. Nothing broken
3. Nothing broken
4. ART
5. Music
6. School
7. Work
8. Travel
9. Sports–Legal
10. Other that could not be listed

Three–Trinity without unity
Above the Law

*"Man separated from Law and Justice,
He is the Worst". – Aristotle*

(Outside of Law and Order)

↓

1. Pursuit of what you want or do
   (Happiness) or action

2. Liberty (includes property & body)
   (Order of Justice)

3. Life (Brackets of Law)
   (Life Low - Low Life)

_____

1. Red Light running
2. Drunk driving
3. Shoplifting
4. Breaking and Entering
5. Assault
6. Bank robbery
7. Identity theft
8. Copyright Infringement
9. Plagiarism
10. Property theft
11. Home invasion
12. Murder
13. Manslaughter
14. Rape
15. Stalking
16. Public or private food tampering
17. Kidnapped
18. Illegal Drug Sales
19. Blackmail – Frauds – Scams
20. Others that could not be listed

**THIS IS NOT MY OPINION AND IT IS NOT A FACT.
THE CHOICE IS YOURS.**

NATURAL SELECTION LAWS

Freedom

Charles Darwin

Natural Selection Law

1. Organism–First (Life)

2. Abilities, talents and traits = Liberty of species

3. Pursuit of survival or action, or the possibility of happiness

4. ~~Reproduction~~ = Not a right, a privilege

Unnatural Selection Law

1. Pursuit of survival or action, or the possibility of happiness

2. Abilities, talents and traits = Liberty of species

3. Organism–Last (Life)

UNDER THE LAW

Who put these in order of checks and balances of law

1. Christ
2. Gandhi
3. Martin Luther King
4. Firefighters
5. Heroes
6. Doctors
7. Pharmacy
8. Most Police Officers
9. Hope
10. Life
11. America Today
12. Peace

ABOVE THE LAW

These are called Low–Life's. They put life last

1. Hitler
2. Stalin
3. Slavery
4. Pyromaniacs
5. Terrorists
6. Murderers
7. Drug Cartel
8. Criminals
9. Suicide
10. Extinction
11. North Korea today
12. War

> The only good ones on this side are the
> -Dare
> -Devils

Respect for organism, no God.

The Line Between

Lack of respect for organism, no God.

10

Charles Darwin

Three–Trinity with unity
Under the Law – (Law made easy)

1. Organism–First (Life)

2. Abilities, talents and traits = Liberty of species

3. Pursuit of survival or action or the possibility of happiness

4. ~~Reproduction~~ = not a right, a privilege

---

1. Regulations for debate within the community of the pursuit of happiness

Branch–Pursuit Branch

Regulations   Ex.   1. Loud Music
               2. Smoking laws
               3. Etc.

---

1. Nothing broken
2. Nothing broken
3. Nothing broken
4. ART
5. Music
6. School
7. Work
8. Travel
9. Sports–Legal
10. Other that could not be listed

Three–Trinity without unity
Above the Law

1. Pursuit of survival or action or the possibility of happiness

2. Abilities, talents and traits = Liberty of species

3. Organism–Last (Life)

---

1. Red Light running
2. Drunk driving
3. Shoplifting
4. Breaking and Entering
5. Assault
6. Bank robbery
7. Identity theft
8. Copyright Infringement
9. Plagiarism
10. Property theft
11. Home invasion
12. Murder
13. Manslaughter
14. Rape
15. Stalking
16. Public or private food tampering
17. Kidnapped
18. Illegal Drug Sales
19. Blackmail – Frauds – Scams
20. Others that could not be listed

TEXT OF HISTORY OF THE CREATOR
THIS IS NOT MY OPINION AND IT IS NOT A FACT.
THE CHOICE IS YOURS.
DECLARATION OF INDEPENDENCE.

Inalienable Rights of Free Will of Freedom.

Endowed by creator
Natural Law

1. Life–Fight for
2. Liberty
3. Pursuit of happiness,
   What they want or
   What they do

Human Rights =
Freedom = Water or
Inalienable Rights =
Free Will =
H_2O Individual

No free will–Free choice
No freedom in land
or domain of free land

Endowed by destroyer
Unnatural Law

1. Pursuit of happiness,
   What they want or
   What they do
2. Liberty
3. Life–Flight from

UNDER THE LAW

Who put these in order of checks
and balances of law

1. Christ
2. Gandhi
3. Martin Luther King
4. Firefighters
5. Heroes
6. Doctors   Good | Evil
7. Pharmacy
8. Most Police Officers
9. Hope
10. Life
11. America Today
12. Peace

ABOVE THE LAW

These are called Low–Life's
They put life last

1. Hitler
2. Stalin
3. Slavery
4. Pyromaniacs
5. Terrorists
6. Murderers
7. Drug Cartel
8. Criminals
9. Suicide
10. Extinction
11. North Korea today
12. War

The only
good ones
on this side
are the
-Dare
-Devils

| Mostly with faith in God or Human Life. | The List Goes On To Life. | **The Line Between Good & Evil.** | The List Goes On To Extinction. | Mostly without faith in God or Human Life. |

Endowed by the creator with faith in God

Match →

They both match equally but, one has faith and one doesn't. Faith with private shaming, less public shaming keeps people under the law more by healing themselves inside instead of taking this anger out on others. Because too much public shaming destroys the soul of the individual that's guilty and sometimes even the innocent.

TEXT OF HISTORY CHARLES DARWIN
THIS IS NOT MY OPINION AND IT IS NOT A FACT.
THE CHOICE IS YOURS.
NATURAL SELECTION LAWS

Freedom
Charles Darwin

Natural Selection Law | Unnatural Selection Law

Natural Selection Law
1. Organism–First (Life)
2. Abilities, talents and traits = Liberty of species
3. Pursuit of survival or action, or the possibility of happiness
4. ~~Reproduction~~ = Not a right, a privilege

Unnatural Selection Law
1. Pursuit of survival or action, or the possibility of happiness
2. Abilities, talents and traits = Liberty of species
3. Organism–Last (Life)

UNDER THE LAW

Who put these in order of checks and balances of law

1. Christ
2. Gandhi
3. Martin Luther King
4. Firefighters
5. Heroes
6. Doctors
7. Pharmacy
8. Most Police Officers
9. Hope
10. Life
11. America Today
12. Peace

ABOVE THE LAW

These are called Low–Life's. They put life last.

1. Hitler
2. Stalin
3. Slavery
4. Pyromaniacs
5. Terrorists
6. Murderers
7. Drug Cartel
8. Criminals
9. Suicide
10. Extinction
11. North Korea today
12. War

The only good ones on this side are the -Dare -Devils

| Respect for organism not God. | The List Goes On To Life. | **The Line Between Good & Evil.** | The List Goes On To Extinction. | Lack of respect for organism or God. |

Match ⟵ Endowed by evolution without faith in God

Evolution without faith naturally having nature's self-conscious or self-control but, with no faith in God. This means or is likely some or less private shaming and more public shaming or collective group ridicule leading to less unity.

TEXT OF LAW OF THE CREATOR

Three–Trinity within unity

Under the Law – (Law made easy)

1. Life (Brackets of Law)
2. Liberty (includes property & body)
3. Pursuit of what you want or do for happiness, or survival

---

1. Regulations for debate within the community of the pursuit of happiness

Branch–Pursuit Branch

	Ex.	1. Loud Music
Regulations		2. Smoking laws
		3. Etc.

---

1. Nothing broken
2. Nothing broken
3. Nothing broken
4. ART
5. Music
6. School
7. Work
8. Travel
9. Sports–Legal
10. Other that could not be listed

Three–Trinity without unity

Above the Law

1. Pursuit of action (Broken brackets of Law)
2. Liberty to protect the persons pursuit of action
3. Life of others last

$$\left(\begin{array}{c}\text{Some only take}\\\text{liberty, not life}\end{array}\right) - \left(\begin{array}{c}\text{Above the law}\\\text{low lives}\end{array}\right)$$

---

1. Red Light running
2. Drunk driving
3. Shoplifting
4. Breaking and Entering
5. Assault
6. Bank robbery
7. Identity theft
8. Copyright Infringement
9. Plagiarism
10. Property theft
11. Home invasion
12. Murder
13. Manslaughter
14. Rape
15. Stalking
16. Public or private food tampering
17. Kidnapped
18. Illegal Drug Sales
19. Blackmail – Frauds – Scams
20. Others that could not be listed

Endowed by the creator with faith in God

Match ──────▶

They both match equally but, one has faith and one doesn't. Faith with private shaming, less public shaming keeps people under the law more by healing themselves inside instead of taking this anger out on others. Because too much public shaming destroys the soul of the individual that's guilty and sometimes even the innocent.

TEXT OF LAW CHARLES DARWING

Three–Trinity with unity

Under the Law – (Law made easy)

1. Organism–First (Life)
2. Abilities, talents and traits = Liberty of species
3. Pursuit of survival or action or the possibility of happiness
4. ~~Reproduction~~ = not a right, a privilege

---

1. Regulations for debate within the community of the pursuit of happiness

Branch–Pursuit Branch

	Ex.	1. Loud Music
Regulations		2. Smoking laws
		3. Etc.

---

1. Nothing broken
2. Nothing broken
3. Nothing broken
4. ART
5. Music
6. School
7. Work
8. Travel
9. Sports–Legal
10. Other that could not be listed

Three–Trinity without unity

Above the Law

1. Pursuit of survival or action or the possibility of happiness
2. Abilities, talents and traits = Liberty of species
3. Organism–Last (Life)

---

1. Red Light running
2. Drunk driving
3. Shoplifting
4. Breaking and Entering
5. Assault
6. Bank robbery
7. Identity theft
8. Copyright Infringement
9. Plagiarism
10. Property theft
11. Home invasion
12. Murder
13. Manslaughter
14. Rape
15. Stalking
16. Public or private food tampering
17. Kidnapped
18. Illegal Drug Sales
19. Blackmail – Frauds – Scams
20. Others that could not be listed

← Match   Endowed by evolution without faith in God

Evolution without faith naturally having nature's self-conscious or self-control but, with no faith in God. This means or is likely some or less private shaming and more public shaming or collective group ridicule leading to less unity.

THE HIDDEN CODE OF GOD
(NATURE'S NATURAL BIBLE OF FREE WILL OR FREE CHOICE)

*L*ife, liberty, and the pursuit of happiness: These are our inalienable rights. Of them, life is first. Without life, there is no liberty or ability to find happiness. Second is liberty. We use our abilities and talents to make a living, to make a life for ourselves, to survive. Sometimes, we take them for granted. Or worse, we take our liberties out on another being. For instance, a purse snatcher who grabs someone's purse in a gas station parking lot. Someone who steals from us is stealing our past—our time.

These are the codes we live by, whether we know it or not. We live by these codes, and these codes overlap with other codes. In this book, we will explore the overlap between our inalienable rights, the law of nature, the law of the land, of life and liberty. Once all the codes are on the table–so to speak–then we'll discuss how easy it is for us to set things right—to live by the codes.

The Structure of Law and Order

Structure is the code. If that doesn't make sense, do not fear; these codes may well be confusing at first, as we begin discussing them, because this is a totally new way of looking at things. But by suspending our disbelief, we begin to have a deeper understanding of these formulas and can actually adjust our lives accordingly.

The structure is simple. Life equals law. Liberty equals order. The pursuit is what you love or what you do. However, law and order are broken when the pursuit of what you love overtakes life or liberty. Liberty is freedom; freedom is liberty. Law and order is life and liberty. That bears repeating: law and order *is* life and liberty. It's just a different word choice for the same thing. Of these, pursuit of happiness is the most powerful thing as it drives our actions. This book will discuss each of these concepts.

The Law of Liberty

While life is the first law to be protected, liberty is second. Laws protect us and our liberties. They protect life. Everyone has this inalienable right. Liberty is a protector of time, abilities, and talents. The law of liberty isn't just about life but what we accumulate with our time. If someone steals property from you, they are stealing your time and taken your liberty.

The Law of Life

Life always comes first. We must have life if we are to have the ability to pursue happiness and/or have love. If someone being deported can prove they will be killed upon deportation, then we don't send them. We grant them asylum. We protect them instead. Another example would be a lawyer whose client says to the lawyer, "I will kill my wife." With this comment, privilege is waived; the lawyer has to report it. In both cases, we protect life. Life always comes first.

Life trumps liberty. Life is protected. And this code is prevalent in every system of our society. *Hipaa. Ferpa.* These laws protect life. Why is jaywalking against the law? The law protects life. When we are driving down the road and see a stop sign, why do we stop? To protect life.

The Law of Love

Love is part of the pursuit. We pursue happiness looking for love. Love trumps all. Through love of self, our motions sometimes merge. It's at these times that love gets distorted into lust, greed, envy, and jealousy. Too often, this is where revenge happens as we look out only for ourselves. Circumventing the process of life, liberty, and the pursuit of happiness, we put our pursuit first as we look for love. The power associated with this may take us above someone else's liberty when we are in this mind-set. We use the pursuit to infringe on others. It's pure selfishness. But when we see love trump all, we can rest assured that love is first.

God's Law = Natural Law

God's law is innate feelings—our free will. Nature's law is in Darwin's code. Therefore, God's law and nature's law are the same things. We have been given our liberty-abilities to pursue our happiness. The master plan centers around survival for the betterment of self and others. This formula must remain as is, in the order of life, liberty, and pursuit of action for happiness, or man becomes his own rule maker over the natural process of life. Flipping this code upside down will eventually will destroy man; mankind will not win over life. Actually, man must never manipulate this code as that could even bring on an unknowing end to our species.

That balance between the laws of the land and natural law happens best when we respect our own lives and the lives of other human beings, when we live within the code of natural law. These codes are the same human rights are the same as inalienable rights are the same or equal to free will. The first human rights reflect our history, inalienable rights represent our structure of laws in the community, and the free will is the code of the Bible of the individual's actions and private sins. All are the same, but all are different checks and balances of humanities destination or path that we are on at that time in our world history.

But God is not perfect, and that may be hard to accept for some people. If God was/is perfect, God would stop learning the changes that the future brings naturally with time. God would also not know the changes that God gave us with our free will or free choice. God has to be imperfect if that free will he gave us is truly free from control.

Christ didn't die to be worshipped. Christ died so that human life could be preserved. Christ died so that we could hold on to our lives and keep lives sacred. Christ died so that our lives were not taken unnaturally by man. Christ's death gives us life. For those who believe and for the nonbelievers as well, nature and God work together to make humanity stronger through failure, suffering, and pain. The human race, through its everlasting struggle, works to preserve human life and to hopefully someday help make life even better.

Patterns of Opposites

These codes are patterns of opposites. The formulas are extreme patterns of history, law, and biblical codes that keep repeating. Individuals are much more complex than just life, liberty, and the pursuit of what we want or do to survive. This is why we can change the formula—depending on our circumstances. We change it to suit our needs at a specific moment in time.

Staying under the Law

No one should put themselves above the law. But no one should stay under the law either. There is a fine balance. Here's a scenario: Someone breaks in to my house; they take my property. They were above the law; they put themselves (their pursuit) above my liberty. In doing this, they have taken my liberty. They are above my liberty. Next, they get arrested. The thief goes to jail. Jail is under the law. Even when they are released, they are under the law. If they break the law again, they will go back under. While on probation or parole, they have to report back to the law, and they remain under it. The more these behavioral patterns continue, the more they shape our history—and ultimately shape our destiny.

MANKIND: THE PROBLEM AND THE SOLUTION

*M*an is the problem and man is the solution, and that is our problem. To solve the problem, the collective and individuals have to work together and respect one another. The collective is a group of people with a common interest.

It's a problem that's a riddle that's a puzzle to our problems that keeps repeating, just like life keeps repeating. It's one of life's catch-22s. But by putting the inalienable rights first, many problems solve themselves. Emotionally driven selfish greed vanishes. Although we will still suffer with the pain of what life naturally brings, the solution to many of life's problems starts with balance of the most important priorities. Put the inalienable rights first, and be careful not to flip the code.

Flipping the Code

Sometimes, we end up misguided. We mistake life, liberty, and the pursuit of action for happiness to survive; we look for another outcome; we want a different result. We become so anxious to get results, we turn the code upside down. During these actions, we don't pursue happiness by the book; we become so desperate that we commit acts of desperation to survive. Whether driven by greed or desperation, our selfishness is above other people's life and liberties; in essence, we take the law into our own hands whenever we flip the code.

Other times, we take the law into our own hands—sometimes with the sole intent to gain power over society at a particular moment in history. A clear sign of a power grab by mankind using government is when the society in power prevents its people from using their liberties or abilities to make practical natural art for survival. In other words, a government that prevents capitalism.

Another clear sign that basic human rights are being violated is when a segment of mankind or a government starts attacking a religious faith or spiritual self-growth even when the attacked person is living within the natural laws and their inalienable rights. Examples include when a government prevents a peaceful protest, when Hitler rose to power, in the beginning of the Cuban revolution (the government kicked the Catholic church out of the country). It's like Marshall law, but it's for the selfish needs of the government.

The Battle of Good and Evil

For every evil act that happens, good happens at a higher rate. That's why evil can never win permanently—unless human life has gone extinct. Maybe the ultimate goal of evil is extinction of the human race. Maybe the daily battles we undergo lead us down the path of annihilation? Respect for human life reduces the chance of extinction and also stalls the evolution of evil.

Evil evolves naturally, and evils rise or evolve together. For instance, the higher the murder rate, the higher the crime, the higher the substance abuse, the suicide rate, abuse of children, abuse of animals, and abuse of fellow humans—they all rise together.

The Good, the people who persuade others not to take human life, can become heroes or savers of other people's lives by putting their own lives at risk for the survival of humanity. The Evil, the controllers and destroyers of society, are often forcing others outside of natural law and their free will. They are the takers of human life for selfish reasons. Maybe they long to control humanity and the people's free will for profit. They use intimidation to dominate society. While these are both forms of natural selection, using force to advance their dominance demonstrates how little respect for laws and human life some people have.

Fight or Flight

People will either fight for life of self in conjunction with humanity or they will flight from life for selfish reasons like love of self—at times, fleeing against humanity. Here's an example: Mankind can become evil by abusing the pursuit of happiness in the form of wants and desires. When we put wants and desires over life, either we destroy ourselves or we have to defend ourselves from the destroyers. Defending ourselves is one example of a "fight for life" stance. Sometimes, we choose to fight for life for survival. The other stance is "flight from life." Sometimes, in order to preserve life, we must flee.

The fighters for human life protect the individual's due process within the law from the group's power. The flighters from human life flee for their own human life to protect the group. This often happens when skipping due process of law. They protect themselves with the group for power. They fight.

Human behavior shaped our history, as it also influenced the creation of moral boundaries that affect our laws and, at times, even our biblical beliefs. But sometimes, these boundaries suffer erosion and our moral compass becomes disconnected from the structure of law. Behavioral responses to fight-or-flight situations have had a significant impact on historical events (e.g., wars, religion, survival). A good example is the Iraq War. Bush went in looking for weapons of mass destruction that he thought were there—he wanted to protect life. He took us in without clear evidence. In time, we learned these weapons were not there. We attempted to solidify the nation. There was much instability in that territory, and when Obama came into the presidency, we pulled out—before the political glue had dried. This is an example of both fight for life and flight to possibly save life.

Sometimes, we want to retreat (flee) and just let things be the way there are. We often actually choose between the two—to fight to defend or to flee to defend. Both are viable options.

Survival of the Fittest

Both fight and fight are part of our survival. The power of people in numbers can answer a threat to ensure survival of the fittest through flight or fight. What this does is to help ensure survival of fittest since it opens options for the survival of human life.

However, anytime this code is broken—the natural code of survival of the fittest—when it's broken for a long time, nature naturally is preprogrammed to declare that thing unfit for nature; it has become unfit to survive, and it will be destroyed as it can no longer stand the test of time. The thing is, compassion for human life is very important, if not the most important virtue for the survival of the human race.

PERFECTION IS IMPOSSIBLE

*P*eople cannot be perfect. Society cannot be perfect. Not even God is perfect. Some of the people, groups, and concepts throughout history who have quested for perfection include: Hitler, ISIS, fascism, socialism, and even political correctness. Life is imperfect. We seek betterment, but evil forces like the devil lie to us, claiming perfection, to lure us into self-destruction. The devil wants to control people's free will, given by God. The devils seek a perfection in society that is unattainable. If nobody's perfect, the quest for perfection is a quest for evil as it seeks to have absolute control over society and eventually, in time, quests for the destruction of that society.

Men or women who seek perfection are bound for destruction. Likewise, when people make God out to be perfect, they will try to impose perfection upon humanity and exert unrealistic control in an attempt to dominate society. But how could people impose perfection upon humanity if God is imperfect? God being imperfect makes it less likely that mankind could impose perfection upon other human beings because perfection is impossible.

Imperfection within the law of free will, given by God or nature, is perfect because we can experiment, make mistakes, and learn from those mistakes, evolving individually to changes that happen within nature.

Self-Reliance

There are five protected classes: impoverished elderly, impoverished children, veterans, the disabled, and the mentally ill. If we are in one of these classes or not self-reliant for another reason, that's when the group is supposed to come in and help us. For the good

24

of humanity, we must help individuals who do not have their own free will. But we have to be careful, too. Once we start taking care of them, we also must be mindful that we don't help them too long—unless they are in one of those five protected classes. Continued assistance takes away their free will; they become dependent on the help and, in turn, the help begins to hinder them.

For instance, the war on poverty isolates people to shelters. This is no mistake. Sometimes, government intends to keep an individual from becoming self-reliant. A lengthy use of government services will strip a person of their self-reliance, sometimes their free will, and sometimes their faith, and eventually, they will be unnaturally reliant on the government instead of on family or faith in self or God. In other words, they will no longer be their own rulers of themselves.

Other times, we impose our will on another country and people using religion. In places such as Iran, Sudan, and Saudi Arabia, religion overpowers the free will of the individual and the individual is stifled in the name of the revolt.

Tolerance of the Masses versus Individualism

Gilbert K. Chesterson said: "Tolerance is the virtue of the man without convictions." This is a code that speaks to both our past and our future. We can see it repeat upon humanity through government force. Politicians decide which laws they will keep and not keep based on their popularity. Their convictions change in order to give the people what they want. It's a form of tolerance. It's also breaking the code.

Using big business' global controls and censorship or politically motivated boycotts to suppress individual rights goes against the virtues of individualism, self-reliance, and people with faith in human life.

But today's definitions of tolerance have changed. We need to have tolerance for our fellow beings—men, women, children, people of color, regardless of sexual orientation—as long as it respects life and the process of making life.

Assets, Greed, and Capitalism

Some animals make assets. Creatures like the bird and the squirrel make a nest to live, but they don't have luggage or other assets to take to the new nest or location. Humans are the only creature that makes assets for trade and that came from the practical art of capitalism for individual survival. Except for humans, animals don't travel or physically transport the assets or property that they make. Except for humans, animals use their assets or tools exclusively at that location for the purpose in that moment.

While all creatures have life, abilities, or liberties to pursue growth, humans are unique in that they make art naturally—which often becomes a human asset. That asset then produces productivity which can be seen as we produce those man-made assets, making up our individual properties, and those properties, collectively, eventually evolve into our economic system, thus creating our monetary system which further advances the trade of those human assets—all in the quest for survival.

Some art is practical; some is capitalistic; some is used for sur-vival. Other art is just creative or beautiful or simply just appreciated. The point is, mankind becomes the creative creator that creates art for survival through capitalism but sometimes just to entertain our-selves. The arts we create are our assets.

Governments tax our assets whether we create them for wealth or pleasure. This taxation can become abused over time and be seen as greed for votes for power. Politicians go beyond the basic collective infrastructure's needs and abuse their power in terms of greed for themselves and for the public survival that has become dependent upon government. Some politicians can and will abuse the tax sys-tem. Some politicians don't really care about taking away our per-sonal liberties or direct liberties like free speech, gun rights, or other inalienable rights—or our assets.

The capitalist system grows from that same equation of life, liberty, and the pursuit of growth that makes useful creative art and in turn that makes products or assets to sell and or trade within the population for survival. All other forms of government: socialist, communist, etc., have to use capitalism in some way or they have to directly abuse free will of their own people or others to fund these collective governments. The exception would be unless the wealth is given or taken from another outside source that funds the communistic or socialistic regimens. Capitalism can become the poor man's ticket out of poverty. That is, unless high taxation, high regulation, and too much union domination negate the productivity. With capitalism, society can create convenience and independence and expand that independence to others who seek prosperity. As long as that capital of capitalism is created using our free will and falls within the law.

Government Power: Chlorine in a Pool

*G*overnment power is like chlorine in a pool—too much will kill life in the pool and too little will cause growth of unwanted bacteria. The basic structure of law and order will breakdown and stifle basic functions that are so needed to maintain productivity and aid in growth of the country. This is also a balancing act of power as a government decides what is best for their constituents. The government decides how much in taxes an individual should pay for collective services like defense of country, roads, schools, parks, etc. These individual costs, or taxes, then pay for those collective services. The only time the individual person should be taxed and transfer wealth outside of defense of country and taxes collectively is when the other individual that the services are transferred to is one of the five exemptions: disabled person, elderly person, veteran, mentally ill person, and children living in poverty. If free will of the individual is transferred to others who have free will who are unwilling, this will, over time, break the code of free will, and that government will eventually run out of other people's wealth, prosperity, and eventually, even property to seize.

Free stuff takes free will from somebody. The old adage: "Nothing is free" rings true here, and eventually, freedom will disappear if it is being abused over and over again. This happens basically because we break the code of survival of the fittest and therefore are then unfit to survive as a nation. Once unfit, a nation (or a people) will be destroyed in time. This usually happens slowly through corruption or when some countries abuse power by overwhelming government force like in Cuba, Venezuela, and North Korea.

The founding fathers of the United States were trying to limit growth of government using the force of government over free will (our inalienable right). They did not want the government to be able to control the individual. Our right to gather, our right to free speech, our right to defend ourselves—the forefathers made sure to protect our inalienable rights from the government.

Socialism, Communism, and Failure

Collective socialist governments consume the individual's possibility for survival of the fittest by smothering their inalienable rights or attempting to alter the natural order of nature's code.

Independence for the individual's own survival can be consumed by a government for the greater good. Forcing a person to pay a fine for not buying health care—for example. It takes away individual free rights. Sometimes, doing something for the greater good does greater harm to the individuals. Still, a group will rally around similar complaints and demand their free will be returned. They will reclaim their rights or consume government itself. This is why socialist governments are the opposite of or in conflict with the declaration of independence of the United States of America. If a government doesn't protect the one person's independent inalienable rights that government eventually cannot protect the whole group of human beings within that country. The whole group is only as strong as the protection of the one individual's inalienable rights, even including wealth and or property belonging to that individual human being.

These socialist forms of government consume too much of the wealth they are trying to create. That is why collective forms of governments have to consume the independence of the individual's inalienable rights. These collective forms of government also cannot produce capital growth well enough to sustain a large country or population. So they eventually abuse free will to hold on to power by desperately doing the most horrendous acts of violence on their own people and sometimes the world. Stalin locked up his people in camps. He broke the law of free will. He preemptively locked people up. He even sent his son to the front lines. He abused the rights of individuals for the power of the government.

Venezuela, North Korea, and Cuba are good examples of this today. They break individual free will or free choice. The most important reason socialism or socialist government's fail is through eliminating survival of the fittest within the individual. When survival of the fittest is broken, nature naturally declares that government as unfit to survive—no longer part of nature's natural order of survival of the fittest, and time will be its demise.

Survival of the fittest is a preprogrammed force of nature using free will of the individual, the source of that survival code. The framers of the constitution unconsciously where reaching that conclusion with creating the declaration of independence first trying to match the declaration of independence and constitution with nature's code of survival of the fittest so that the survival of the individual has the best chance of survival. Therefore, in turn, the country had the best chance to survive or last as long as the constitution was kept by matching nature's code of survival of the fittest match with the individual. Granting priority to the individual the declaration of independence to survive without governments overwhelming force or dominance becoming the almighty power over our individual lives. Political science today is somewhat the same as it was long ago it is the balance between collective state and the individual's freedom. This will not change even with force the inalienable rights will still be there searching for freedom or a free land to pursue their free will. Sometimes, a free will people go outside of the law and that is the only time when force of government is needed if that individual breaks the laws of natural law within free will. This is a difficult balancing act, respecting the citizen's free will within the laws and of the state's laws to maintain law and order. The citizen's free will must be respected to have sustainable growth in any land that proclaims itself to be a land of freedom.

Socialism, communism, and the other collective forms of governments will always fail in time because those forms of government are not meant for humans. Socialism implemented faithfully only works in the insect world like ants, bees, and termites. They work as a colony or a collective organism each having a predesigned mission without individual free will or with not much of any choice. Most importantly, socialism and communism consume too much of the wealth that it is trying to create.

Basically, too many dollars are consumed in the process of making economic energy for growth in the beginning processes of the vast government consumption of that wealth. Collective perfection of socialism and communism destroy society in time while individual betterment grows the society with respect for human life and law and order. It takes a system of due process to make sincere progress over time. It takes hard work by the individual using his/her own free will not force to make true prosperity within any country.

Darwin and the Declaration

Natural selection, the theory introduced by Charles Darwin, is in a sense, the same as the Declaration of Independence of the United States of America. The two systems align like this: life is an organism; liberty is the abilities, talents, and traits of a species; the pursuit of happiness is the quest for survival of that species. They are the same code.

The Government as a Weapon

Basically, everyone is selfish. It is a natural human trait. Though we try to balance, we often see emotional selfishness surface in groups of people—people who love power and control and who wish to further their agenda. We find power in the form of groups. The government has power and influence—**and can use those qualities to make change. People who want something changed, go to the government. For instance, in California recently, the people voted on Prop 8. They voted down gay marriage. Special-interest groups went around the will of the people (the voters) and went through the court, and the court ruled to overturn the ruling and allowed the marriages over the process of making life. The people were able to use their government to make change sometimes at the expense of the public's will.**

Sometimes, the people even use government as a weapon. Say, a group gathers for activism around a cause—they have a need they want to solve. They rally. They try to manipulate the situation. They want what they want over someone else's free will. In that way, the public has a lot of power. If we go to our congressman for change in groups, sheer numbers can create action—after all, the congressman will want to be reelected, so they will often act. Sometimes, they request that an ad be pulled due to their outrage; sometimes, they pressure private enterprise to remove an item from inventory. Both are forms of forced lobbying; even if the group is in the minority, they have more power in how loud their voices have become to influence the politicians.

These actions may offer a type of control that some people desperately lack and yearn for in their own lives. But we must be careful. The government is not always on the side of the people. Say, the government wants to take your assets or wealth, which are your indirect liberties that you have accumulated over time from using your direct liberties (your body, mind, abilities, and talents). This sometimes happens by overtaxing the taxpayer in order to grow power for themselves and their groups. Some government services use government as a business and profess that government growth is the answer. They will try to convince us that our own problems can all be solved by government growth. This isn't altruism; this approach furthers their agenda and their control over the individual.

Evolving to Exist

*P*erfection in life is impossible. Why? It defeats the purpose of the mission of life, which is survival of the fittest. If it is perfect, it no longer fits into nature's survival of the fittest. That perfect thing has taken itself out of the natural order of betterment for survival and therefore becomes unfit for survival. Darwin's code of survival of the fittest and of natural selection matches nature's evolutionary process—life to survive. And the Declaration of Independence of the United States matches nature's evolutionary process—life to survive.

Therefore, what stops evolving or growing must be dead or in the process of decline for that natural process of evolution to stop evolving and adapting naturally to changes that happen in life. Something that's perfect would not have to change anymore to adapt; if it's perfect, it doesn't need to adapt.

Time does not stand still; therefore, life does not stand still. It evolves daily, and evolution evolves all species through all time adapting to all of nature's changes. This evolution must happen for nature to even exist. People are nature, and we must keep evolving and changing for growth in order to adapt to the survival of fittest using nature.

Empathy for Others

Intelligence does not always equal compassion and poverty does not equal violence; it is disrespecting human life and liberty in general that will make some always equal evil. The lack of faith in human life or empathy toward others becomes the driving force of most violence today. Maybe the answer is helping good-hearted people to become more compassionate rather than trying to help intelligent people to be good-hearted which risks situations with less empathy toward others.

Faith

God is real for many people. I am not religious and never have been, probably will never be in the classical sense, but even I can see that God is real; most people are good; some people are naive; people can be all-too-easily persuaded to do bad deeds.

A God that has faith in human life is real for the betterment of mankind, and God is the gift of life and a reality around us every day in ourselves and within others.

A Good God

A good God gives life naturally and takes life naturally; an evil God takes life unnaturally (mankind could be considered an evil God at times when he takes life unnaturally). That's why it's better to give than it is to take in life. Selfishness sometimes can and will become a person's own worst enemy, if that selfishness becomes void of a God or denies respect for human life and the liberty of others. It's just the way it works.

Some humans need a foundation of moral guidance that respects the process of natural life to be good and have respect for others. This is not the case for all people, but the population as a whole is better off with faith in human life, guidance from the family, and a family compass rooted in respect for God and life.

Love Is Love Is Love

Love is one of the most rewarding emotions in life—if the quest for that love is managed or controlled properly. The quest for love will continue throughout life until love is found or until life becomes more important and is at risk of being lost. Until that point, love is the one specific thing people search for most in life. If the emotion of love is not managed properly, it morphs and is changed into jealousy or revenge or greed. When love morphs within a person, that person tries to take what they want or need from others. They do this by declaring themselves a victim. But then they go on the offense and become the victimizer looking for power. People operating under this formula take other people's property (an indirect liberty) or their body (a direct liberty). Some self-medicate instead and get lost in addiction to drugs or alcohol instead of victimizing others. This poor lifestyle choice is not and will never be a permanent fix. Rarely does it even work in the short term. Thankfully, most people come out of that mind-set and put their lives in a better perspective. Their own life and others' lives gradually become the focus, overtaking love of self. But if this code is broken—if more and more people choose selfishness over altruism—we will actually increase the chance of extinction for the human race. That bears repeating: life, liberty, and the pursuit of happiness for survival will, over time, exacerbate the possibility of our demise. The formula provided herein offers us a checks and balance; it works on an individual life, and it works for humanity as a whole.

The Purity of the Spirit

Faith in God translated for the nonreligious is hope in life. Therefore, God with nature made man and then man-made art, art made man better—that's why man makes art—**to hopefully change other people's hearts. Anything that breaks God's code of nature will go extinct in time—and that includes mankind. If this code is broken, it can only be temporarily broken, and it can only be broken for self-defense. Otherwise, it's nature's natural code to preserve life.**

God wins when human life wins; man loses when human life loses. Human life must win for man to win. Jesus, the spirit of the life, protects the soul and the mind from the pollution that man can bestow. The spirit remains pure to matter how polluted the soul becomes or how dominant the pollution of the soul can be. The spirit of life will always try to bring the soul back—to protect it from its pursuit of happiness when that pursuit takes over life in the spirit of God. By having faith in God, we have hope in life.

Respect the Code / Respect Life

What it all means is that we may be looking at the actual Jesus code of law, made by the creator. These formulas teach us how to live by the code. They prove that living by the code grants us our survival. If we live by the code, we will survive. Not respecting human life leads all of humanity down a very dark road—perhaps even mass death. The good news is: there's still time. There is still time for each and every one of us. Good survival of the fittest preserves human life; bad survival of the fittest takes human life unless in defense of preserving human life naturally.

Follow the code of the creator that creates life.

ABOUT THE AUTHOR

*W*hen Matt Asher was but five years old, his father hand-built a camper and moved the family to Mexico. They spent a year traveling and living off the land. The abrupt changes in lifestyle caused culture shock for Matt. As a form of protection, Matt turned inward.

Through this inward-looking lens, Matt Asher started looking for truth.

He has no intent to make money or profit from this project. He uses his free will—sometimes incorrectly—but always striving to change for the better. He learned so much through his researching for answers, he felt compelled to help others by writing this book.

He is hopeful that this information will help make many lives better. Matt says he has God to thank for helping him to see these formulas, and he feels this information will help others down a similar path to balance.

"AT HIS BEST, MAN IS THE NOBLEST OF ALL ANIMALS; SEPARATED FROM LAW AND JUSTICE HE IS THE WORST"

—ARISTOTLE

This is a very personal story, but it's based on logic rather than emotion. It's a story that should help all of us destroy the bad emotions that lurk inside us.

This is how we will survive.

One day, while mowing the lawn, I had an epiphany. This flash of truth just came naturally like a flash of light, and from that first flash, I felt as though I had been given the formula of humanity.

Starting that night, while I tried to sleep, something kept pushing at me and waking me up. The spirit would not let me sleep. It pushed at me over and over again. I finally gave in, got up, and the spirit helped me write out the formula for free-will.

I could never have done this alone.

I opened up my mind and began to take note of everything. Things that made sense, things that didn't. I then filtered those things down—little by little—taking out opinion and leaving just what I knew to be true.

The inner spirit was guiding me on my journey. It was attempting to help me clean my own soul after years of neglect. I was convinced that this happened because the spirit wanted me to be content with myself. It wanted me to seek truth. The truth would allow me to grow.

The truth will allow us to grow.

After flipping the formula of humanity upside down, I then flipped free will upside down. When that happened, the flood gates of truth from the creator and the destroyer opened up. History, law, the bible, and all that makes up human behavior. It all became clear.

We are human behavior.